Mountains

ENDANGERED PEOPLE & PLACES

Mountains

BY NEIL STRONACH

Photographs by Still Pictures

Lerner Publications Company • Minneapolis

All words that appear in **bold** are explained in the glossary on page 46.

Map by European Map Graphics Ltd. Artwork by Mike Atkinson. Photographs on pp. 22, 28-29, 36, 37 by ZEFA Picture Library; all other photographs by Still Pictures.

This edition first published in the United States in 1996 by Lerner Publications Company, 241 First Avenue North, Minneapolis, MN 55401.
Copyright © 1995 Cherrytree Press Ltd.

Library of Congress Cataloging-in-Publication Data
Stronach, Neil.
    Mountains / by Neil Stronach.
        p.   cm. — (Endangered people and places)
    Includes index.
    Summary: Discusses mountain people, climate, landscape, plants, animals, and present and future threats to them.
        ISBN 0-8225-2777-4 (lib. bdg. : alk. paper)
    1. Mountain people—Juvenile literature. 2. Mountains—Juvenile literature.
3. Mountain ecology—Juvenile literature. [1. Mountains. 2. Mountain life. 3. Mountain ecology. 4. Ecology.] I. Title. II. Series.
GF57.S77   1996
333.73—dc20   95-25400
                                                                                CIP
                                                                                AC

Printed in Italy by L.E.G.O. s.p.a., Vicenza
Bound in the United States of America
1 2 3 4 5 6 01 00 99 98 97 96

CONTENTS

UNDERSTANDING MOUNTAINS

About 20 percent of the earth's habitable surface lies at more than 3,280 feet (1,000 meters) above sea level. Most of this land is made up of mountains. It contains some of the harshest conditions for life. Steep hills and extreme cold can make mountain living difficult for all creatures. But over the centuries, the inhabitants of mountain regions have developed ways of making the best out of difficult circumstances.

Almost since time began, people from lowland areas have both feared and revered mountains. Until the 1800s, Europeans thought of mountains as wild, dangerous places with backward and warlike inhabitants. It was not until about 200 years ago that visitors began traveling in mountain areas and climbing peaks. They learned about the lives of mountain people and studied the mountain environment. Today, we tend to think of mountains as beautiful places, ideal for vacations and recreation.

But contact with the modern world has also brought many threats to mountains and their people. Environmental and social change, war, and tourism all pose problems. So do the actions of people who do not understand the fragile balance of nature in mountainous areas. But it is not too late. The example of mountain people can help us find ways to save these precious places.

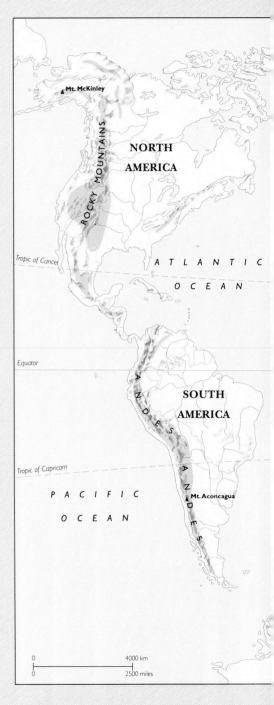

Above: A map of the world, showing mountainous areas over 5,000 feet (1,500 m). Mountains are formed when two of the **plates** that make up the earth's **crust** collide with each other. Over millions of years, these massive plates buckle and fold to form mountains.

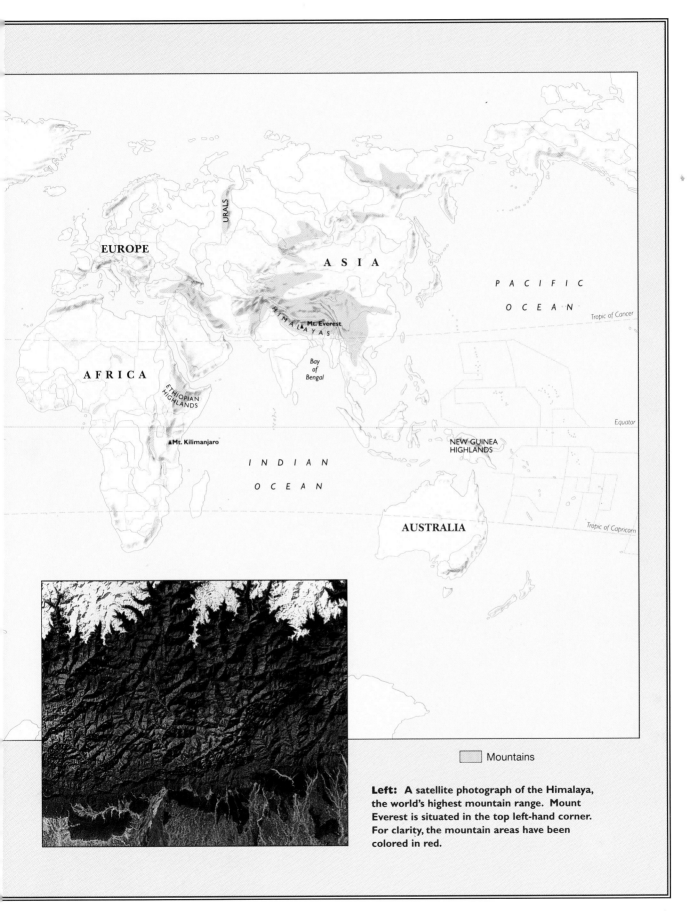

EUROPE

ASIA

AFRICA

URALS

HIMALAYAS ▲Mt. Everest

Bay
of
Bengal

ETHIOPIAN
HIGHLANDS

▲Mt. Kilimanjaro

INDIAN

OCEAN

PACIFIC

OCEAN

Tropic of Cancer

NEW GUINEA
HIGHLANDS

Equator

AUSTRALIA

Tropic of Capricorn

☐ Mountains

Left: A satellite photograph of the Himalaya, the world's highest mountain range. Mount Everest is situated in the top left-hand corner. For clarity, the mountain areas have been colored in red.

HOW MOUNTAINS FORM

The earth is a ball of hot melted rock with a solid skin, or crust. Like currents in the ocean, movements in the molten, or liquid, rock cause the crust to crack into plates. The globe has eight major plates plus a few smaller ones. Currents beneath these plates push them, causing them to move constantly.

Moving Plates
Plate movements are extremely slow. The fastest plates move only 4 inches (10 centimeters) a year. But the results of the movements are easy to see. When the plates collide, the earth's crust is wrinkled up into **fold mountains.** The Himalaya were formed when the Indian plate pushed northward against the continent of Asia. The crust was forced upward into high mountains. The

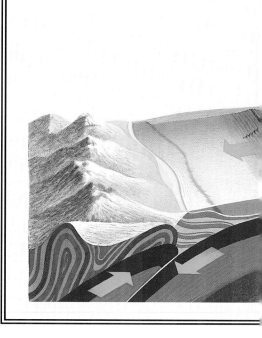

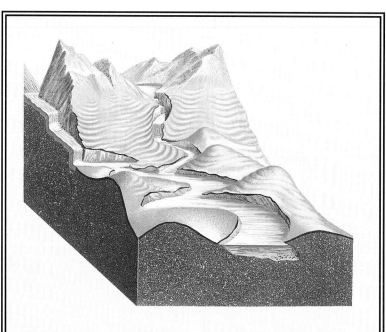

THE WORK OF WATER

Water is one of the main forces that shapes mountains. It collects high up in the form of snow and ice. As water melts and rushes down a mountainside, the torrent carves waterfalls and gorges in the rock. Farther down, as more water enters the stream, it becomes a river. The river moves more slowly, washing away the high ground on its banks and creating a **valley.** As the river swings from side to side, it widens the valley.

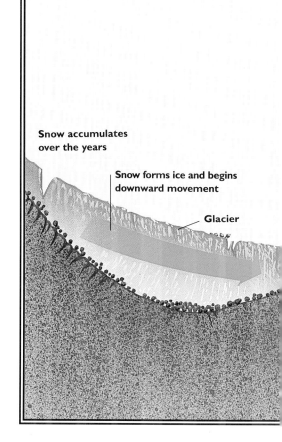

Snow accumulates over the years

Snow forms ice and begins downward movement

Glacier

PLATES ON THE MOVE

When two plates move apart, water flows in to fill the space, forming an ocean. When two plates collide, they either make a trench or form mountains. As the colliding sections of crust crumple and fold, weak points widen into cracks. The descending plate melts in the heat beneath the crust. Some of this melted material, called magma, rises through the cracks and reaches the earth's surface through **volcanoes.** This is happening in places such as the Andes Mountains of South America.

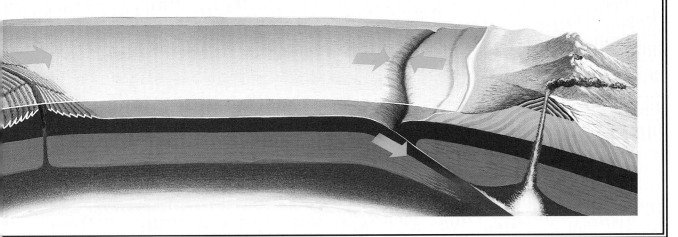

THE ACTION OF ICE

As a glacier moves down a mountainside, it collects small rocks that carve out a valley. At the end of the valley, the rocks carried by the glacier are dumped, forming a mass called a **moraine.**

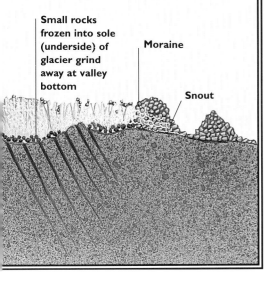

Small rocks frozen into sole (underside) of glacier grind away at valley bottom

Moraine

Snout

Indian plate is still moving northward 2 inches (5 cm) a year, and the Himalaya are still rising.

Some plate movements cause cracks that allow the molten rock to come to the surface. This process creates volcanoes, such as Mount Kilimanjaro in Africa. Here, some of the land along the crack has risen and other sections have dropped, forming **block mountains** with steep sides.

Erosion

At the same time mountains are rising, they are also being worn down by water and wind. This process, called **erosion,** gives mountains their characteristic features. In the highest mountains, water falls as snow. The snow collects and forms rivers of ice called **glaciers.** As a glacier moves downhill, it carves through the rock and creates valleys. At the glacier's **snout,** melting water from the glacier forms a river that continues the process of erosion.

Over time, erosion is a powerful force. The hills of Scotland are the remnants of a mountain range that, millions of years ago, was the size of the Himalaya. The Himalaya, as the world's youngest mountains, have barely begun to be eroded.

THE EFFECTS OF ALTITUDE

Many of the special conditions on mountains are caused by their height—or **altitude**—above sea level. As you climb a mountain, the air gets cooler. It cools about 3° F (5° C) with each increase of 1,000 feet (300 m) in altitude. On a high mountain, such as Mount Everest (29,028 ft/8,848 m) in the Himalaya, the air can become extremely cold.

The higher you climb, the thinner the air becomes. Thinner air has less oxygen. To get enough oxygen to breathe, mountain animals such as yaks and llamas have especially large hearts and lungs. Thin air also holds less

moisture, making the air very dry. And the thin air on high mountains does not filter out as many of the sun's rays, so people can get sunburned more easily. Surfaces such as rocks and leaves can heat up rapidly. When the sun goes behind a cloud or sets for the night, these surfaces cool very quickly.

Rainfall and Drought

Warm winds from the lowlands and the sea rise when they meet the mountains. As the air rises, it gets cooler. Then moisture in the air condenses to form clouds. The moisture falls as rain. Rainfall is greatest at about 6,500 feet (2,000 m). Above this altitude there is less rain.

Rain often falls mainly on one side of a mountain. The other side, called the mountain's **rain shadow,** is much drier. The Andes, the Rockies, and the Himalaya throw very big rain shadows. At the highest altitudes, moisture falls as snow.

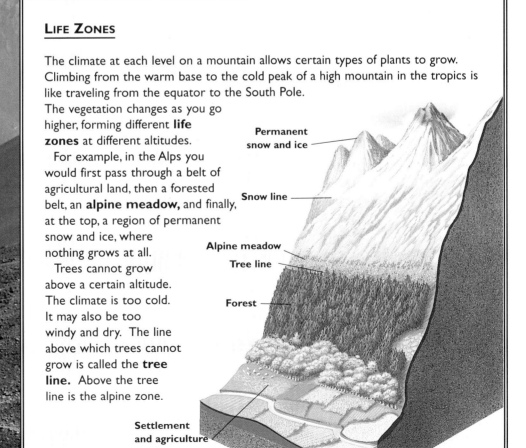

LIFE ZONES

The climate at each level on a mountain allows certain types of plants to grow. Climbing from the warm base to the cold peak of a high mountain in the tropics is like traveling from the equator to the South Pole.

The vegetation changes as you go higher, forming different **life zones** at different altitudes.

For example, in the Alps you would first pass through a belt of agricultural land, then a forested belt, an **alpine meadow,** and finally, at the top, a region of permanent snow and ice, where nothing grows at all.

Trees cannot grow above a certain altitude. The climate is too cold. It may also be too windy and dry. The line above which trees cannot grow is called the **tree line.** Above the tree line is the alpine zone.

Permanent snow and ice

Snow line

Alpine meadow

Tree line

Forest

Settlement and agriculture

MOUNTAIN PLANTS AND ANIMALS

The plants and animals that live at high altitudes have learned to cope with extreme conditions. This process is called adaptation. But at the same time, they can be damaged easily. Mountain plants grow more slowly and reproduce with greater difficulty than those that live in milder environments. And because they are separated from each other, different mountain ranges may shelter species that are found nowhere else. Many mountain species are extremely rare.

Above: Large predatory animals, such as this grizzly bear, are usually the first to be killed off by humans. But some survive in remote mountain areas, such as the Rockies of North America. In the lowlands grizzlies have mostly disappeared.

Mountain Animals

Animals, too, have adapted to withstand the harsh conditions. The yak and snow leopard of central Asia have warm coats that protect them from the extreme cold. The wild goats (markhor and ibex) of the

MOUNTAIN PLANTS

Right: The edelweiss is a typical alpine plant. Its cushion-like growth form protects it from strong winds and from the nibbling of mountain animals. It can grow on the scanty, rocky soils that are common in the alpine zone of Asian and European mountains. The leaves are leathery and hairy to help hold in water. The hairs also protect the plant.

Left: The colorful flowers of many alpine plants, such as this dianthus, attract insects for pollination.

Right: A great variety of alpine flowers grows on the banks of the River Po, Italy's longest river, near its source in the Alps. Farther downstream, a dam uses much of the water from the river to generate **hydroelectric power.**

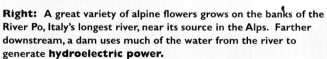

Below: The lammergeier is a mountain vulture that lives in Europe, Asia, and Africa. It has a wingspan of 10 feet (3 m). It feeds on the bones of dead mountain animals. On finding a bone, the bird drops the bone from a height onto a rock. When the bone shatters, the lammergeier eats the splinters, which its powerful stomach can digest.

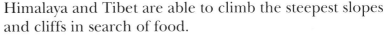

Himalaya and Tibet are able to climb the steepest slopes and cliffs in search of food.

Very few insects and other cold-blooded creatures live on high mountains. But the Himalaya have insects that live in the snow. They feed on the bodies of other insects that strong winds have carried up from the lowlands. These snow insects have adapted so well to the cold that even the warmth of a human hand will kill them.

Animal Migrations

Mountains do not always provide animals with all their needs. The Andean condor is a huge vulture that nests in the mountains of Peru. Each day condors fly to the ocean shore to feed on dead fish and fur seals. Such regular journeys are called **migrations.**

Mountain animals often migrate uphill in spring and back down in autumn. They can find rich feeding in the mountain forests and alpine meadows during summer and then return to warmer altitudes down below for the winter. Bears and rodents do not migrate. They sleep during the winter instead.

Grazing animals, such as wild sheep, dislike the deep snow that collects in the valleys each winter. The argalis of the Pamirs, for example, migrate to high dry mountains where strong winds keep the slopes clear of snow even in winter.

LIVING ON MOUNTAINS

Mountains present a big challenge to the people who live on them. Steep mountain slopes make even basic activities like farming and traveling difficult. Most people travel on rough tracks. They either walk or ride on the backs of animals. Loads are carried either by the people themselves or by pack animals, such as yaks and llamas. The **Sherpa** people of Nepal regularly carry loads that are almost as heavy as themselves.

River Crossings

Swift rivers flow through steep mountain valleys and gorges. These rivers can be dangerous, and people have invented many ways of crossing them. Wide rivers that are not too swift may be crossed by swimming the pack animals to the other side. Simple ferries are made of floating animal skins that have been blown up like balloons. Narrow gorges may be crossed by rope bridges or by baskets suspended on ropes by pulleys.

Terrace Cultivation

In order to plant crops, farmers clear land of its natural vegetation. In doing so, they expose the bare soil. In mountain areas, soil erodes very easily. Rain washes it down a slope. Eventually, there will be no soil left to grow crops.

Above: Densely populated areas of Nepal were once forested. Now they support farmers. To help protect the soil on steep slopes from erosion, the land is terraced, as in this picture. But making terraces is hard work and takes time. Usually, villagers work together to maintain each other's terraces. Such collaboration needs a strong, unified community.

Making **terraces** solves several problems at once. Terraces are long banks, or steps, of soil that hug the slope of a mountain. Stone walls hold the soil in place. Terraces prevent rainwater from rushing down the slope, taking the soil with it. They also provide a flat surface for agricultural work.

Terraces help thirsty crops grow by keeping the water in the soil longer. The terraces are built on slopes that face the sun. The people, too, like to make the best of the sun by living in small villages near their crops.

Mountain Villages

In some places, villages seem to be clinging dangerously to steep mountain slopes. But such villages are usually better sited there than in the valley bottoms. Although the soil is usually richer at the base of the valley, only wide, low valleys get enough sun to make cultivation possible on the valley floor.

Above: Rope bridges look flimsy but are strong enough to bear the weight of whole flocks of sheep and goats. They are ideal for spanning deep, narrow river gorges, such as this one in Nepal. The materials for these bridges are all available in the mountains. This herdsman has used red dye to identify his sheep.

Left: The Taksang Monastery, one of the oldest in Bhutan, perches on a cliff face. This Buddhist monastery was built here for protection from attack. The mountains of central Asia have a long history of war. The monks and local villagers could take shelter in the monastery when their enemies raided.

CROSSING GORGES

Mountains are frequently cut by steep valleys and gorges. These are very difficult to cross. In the Himalaya, people have designed ways of crossing rivers using only the simplest of materials. Narrow gorges can be bridged using only a single tree trunk. Simple bridges use several tree trunks tied together.

Rope bridges can span wider gorges. This river in Bhutan is bridged with a basket on a rope. The basket is pulled across the gorge with another rope. Such a lightweight bridge can easily be taken down if enemies threaten.

MIGRATIONS

Like the plants and animals, mountain people make full use of the different life zones on the slopes. They keep livestock, such as sheep or cows, and herd them up to the rich pastures in the alpine zone in the summer.

In the winter, livestock are often brought into the houses and fed hay and grain grown on the nearby terraces. The warmth of the animals' bodies helps heat the houses. In Nepal, a layer of snow on the roof also provides insulation from the cold.

Transhumance

When people and their livestock follow the seasons up and down the mountain, the migration is called **transhumance.** Transhumance is practiced mostly in the Himalaya, in the Atlas Mountains of North Africa, and in the Alps and the Pyrenees of Europe.

Yak Herders of Dolpo

Sometimes the people who lead this way of life will trade with villagers along the way. In some cases, like that of the Buddhist yak herders of Dolpo, the trade becomes important for their survival.

Dolpo, in northern Nepal, is in the rain shadow of the Himalaya. The low rainfall means that the people of Dolpo, known as Dolpo-pa, cannot grow enough grain to last them the whole year. Once a year, in July, they travel north to Tibet with their yak caravans. There, they exchange barley and corn for salt before returning home. In October, the Dolpo-pa travel south with their salt on a journey that takes three weeks and is full of dangers. They head for the villages of the Rong-pa, a Hindu people, who grow plenty of grain but lack

Below: This farmer from a nomadic community in Kashmir carries a plow. In spring some of these people migrate to the high pastures with their herds. Others stay behind to grow crops. This division of labor ensures a continuous supply of food throughout the year.

16

Right: Government officials often ignore **deforestation** of mountains, even when it is caused by illegal logging for timber. The voices of the mountain people are also ignored. Such neglect is the cause of many problems faced by mountains and their people.

salt for their sheep and goats. The Dolpo-pa trade their salt for the grain of the Rong-pa.

The Dolpa-pa spend the winter on the pastures of the Rong-pa. The latter, meanwhile, begin their own migration, with their sheep and goats, to the Himalayan foothills of southern Nepal. There, they trade beans for Indian salt before returning home.

Below: Herders in Tibet move their livestock to rich summer pastures, often far from their villages. Summer pastures are usually situated in areas that cannot be cultivated. The herders live in camps. Winter forces them to return to their villages.

17

FRONTIERS AND WARFARE

Because mountain ranges present such rugged barriers, they often form boundaries between nations. For example, in South America the Andes form the border between Chile and Argentina. In Africa, the Kivu Mountains separate Rwanda from Uganda and Zaire. In the Himalaya and neighboring ranges, several nations border each other—India, Pakistan, Afghanistan, Tajikistan, China, Nepal, Bhutan, and Myanmar.

Mountain Borders

Governments set up frontier offices for the business of immigration and customs. The local people often ignore these regulations because the borders cut across their traditional lands. For example, the migration routes of the Kyrgyz people have been cut by the borders between Afghanistan and Tajikistan, making it difficult for them to follow their traditional way of life.

The Pathans, who live on the mountainous border between Pakistan and Afghanistan, have always ignored the national border. In the mountains of Peru and of Kurdistan, governments have been fighting long guerrilla wars with the independent-minded inhabitants. Such fighting makes it difficult to address other serious problems that mountains face.

Below: A mullah (Islamic religious leader) leads Afghan guerrillas in prayer. The war that began with the Soviet invasion of Afghanistan did not end when the Russians finally withdrew. Rival Afghan groups continued fighting among themselves. In such situations, young people grow up knowing no way of life other than fighting.

War

The greatest problems of all arise when arguments between nations lead to war. If war is declared, the mountains become battlefields. Even in peacetime, soldiers in Khunjerab and Taxkorgan **National Parks** in the Pamirs killed most of the rare Marco Polo sheep for meat.

In the years since World War II, there have been many other wars, smaller in scale but in many cases still terribly destructive to mountainous regions. Tibet has been invaded by China. India and Pakistan have fought a bitter war in the Himalayan state of Kashmir. The Soviet Union invaded Afghanistan, and a bloody war began that has continued for many years. There have been several civil wars in Ethiopia. And the Kurds, who live in the mountains bordering Iran, Iraq, and Turkey, have suffered severely from a series of wars in Iraq.

Left: Centuries of land abuse and war have left the people of the Ethiopian highlands with a difficult way of life. They have built their villages and monasteries on flat hilltops to defend them from raiders. On these high plateaus they grow scanty crops and raise sheep and cattle.

National parks have been created in the Semien and Balé mountains to help people and wildlife live together. But these and other recent projects have failed in the face of war. Not only have the people lost out, but so have such unique Ethiopian animals as the mountain nyala, Ethiopian wolf, and walia ibex.

Apart from the obvious dangers, war also brings terrible hardships to people whose lives are already difficult. In 1979, when the Soviet Union invaded Afghanistan, many Kyrgyz people of the Afghan Pamirs left their mountain homes. They were forced to live in a refugee camp in Pakistan. There, many died of disease. Now they live in Turkey, far from their native land. They are unlikely ever to return.

Above: Surrounded by reels of barbed wire, a Kurdish boy wades in a stream in a refugee camp. War in Iraq has forced many Kurds to leave their homes and enter Turkey. Here, they live in refugee camps that depend on aid from other countries.

MOUNTAINS AND PEOPLE

Until recently, mountain people followed a way of life that was well adapted to their environment. They understood that the mountain environment was fragile, and they were careful not to use it beyond its limits. In general, the relationship between population and resources was balanced and stable.

Culture and Tradition

Human culture and tradition played an important role in this balance. The knowledge, rules, and customs shared by a group of people was handed down from generation to generation. The people followed the traditional knowledge accumulated by previous generations through a centuries-long process of trial and error. Such traditions covered farming methods, rules for sharing communal resources such as land, and practices for controlling family and population size. All this helped keep a good, or sustainable, balance with the environment.

Modernity and Change

Contact with the modern world has brought about rapid and wide-ranging change, with drastic results on the culture and traditions of mountain peoples. The changes have been physical, such as roads, dams, mining, or forestry. They have also been social and economic—new patterns of work and trade. Once these changes are set in motion, the delicate balance between culture and environment is upset and both suffer.

Left: The village of Wandiphodrang, Bhutan, nestles on a mountain slope. On the cultivated terraces below the village grow the crops that feed the people.

Below: The village of Gulmit in the Hunza Valley of Pakistan. In these rugged mountains, farmland is scarce. There is little rain because most falls on the other side of the Himalaya. The water in the river comes mainly from melting snow and ice.

21

THE ANDES

After the Himalaya, the Andes Mountains form the second largest mountain chain in the world. They run like a backbone along the Pacific coast of South America. They stretch for 4,500 miles (7,250 kilometers), from Venezuela in the north to Chile in the far south.

About two-thirds of the chain is within the tropics. Overall, the Andes contain the greatest variety of environments of any mountain range in the world. These vary from sub-Antarctic to tropical rain forest, and from active volcanoes to high-altitude desert.

Home of the Incas

The Andes were home to the Inca Empire, which flourished for 300 years until 1532. The Incas were expert engineers. They built terraces and **irrigation** systems for growing maize (corn). They also developed ways to store large quantities of food, in case the unpredictable weather of the Andes destroyed their crops. They made beautiful jewelry from gold and silver. They built large cities, roads, and bridges with a skill that is still admired today.

Sadly, the Inca Empire was destroyed by Spanish invaders in 1532. The people of the Andes were enslaved by their new Spanish masters.

ANDES LIFE ZONES

The eastern slopes of the Andes are so high that they cover a number of climatic zones. At each level, the people grow the crops that are best adapted to the altitude. For example, on the lower slopes they grow coffee and maize, which need a warmer climate, while cattle graze in the cooler zones higher up the mountain.

Land of Frost

Snow Line
Some grazing and agriculture at lowest altitudes
10,000 ft (3,000 m)

Cold Land

Potatoes
Vegetables
Dairy farming
Villages
6,000 ft (1,800 m)

Temperate Land

Coffee
Maize
Fruit
3,000 ft (900 m)

Hot Land

Rain forest

The Andes Today

Rainfall is highest on the eastern side of the Andes, where present-day inhabitants take advantage of the different life zones there. They farm potatoes and vegetables at one level and coffee, fruit, and maize lower down. This practice helps spread the risk if a crop at one particular level should fail.

In Peru and Bolivia, the mountain range widens to form a series of high-altitude plateaus flanked by two lines of peaks. These plateaus are known collectively as the **altiplano.** Lying at more than 10,000 feet (3,000 m) above sea level, the altiplano supports the largest high-altitude population in the world. About 7.5 million people live here, growing potatoes and barley. Their animals—llamas and alpacas—graze all year up to the snow line. The potato, which originally came from the Andes, is grown at up to 13,700 feet (4,200 m).

In many ways, the people of the Andes are less well off today than they were at the time of the Incas. Population growth means that more people are trying to feed themselves from the same amount of land. Poverty, soil erosion, deforestation, and overgrazing are the result.

Above: Present-day descendants of the Incas with their llamas, among Incan ruins in Peru, South America. Llamas, which are used for carrying loads, were first domesticated about 6,500 years ago. These relatives of the camel are better suited to life in the Andes than horses and cattle are.

Right: At 12,600 feet (3,800 m) above sea level, Lake Titicaca is the highest large lake in the world. It was once a center of the Inca Empire. Today the pastures on its shores are overgrazed. The lake is slowly drying out, and nearby mines pollute the water and fish. These problems threaten the livelihoods of the local Uru people. These fishermen live on floating islands made from the totora reeds that grow in the lake shallows. The people also make boats and rafts from the reeds.

THE ALPS

The Alps are western Europe's most extensive mountain system. They are 600 miles (965 km) long from east to west. From the very earliest times, events in the Alps have been closely linked with those in the rest of Europe.

The Alps have formed an important cultural barrier between Europe's southern, Mediterranean regions and the countries to the north. Long ago, alpine people were generally self-sufficient, obtaining their food from the crops they grew and the animals they kept.

Right: The effects of **acid rain** on trees in the Alps near Grande Chartreuse in France. Chemical pollution in the atmosphere, especially from power stations, damages and kills forests.

Below: Sheep graze on a high-altitude pasture in a traditional alpine farm. In many parts of the Alps, communities have abandoned farming for more profitable ways of using the land, such as for winter sports.

Beginning around 1850, regions that had better growing conditions began to compete with alpine agriculture. In many areas, alpine inhabitants stopped farming and moved instead to the cities of the lowlands, where the number of jobs in factories was growing rapidly. As farmers left, other parts of the alpine economy, such as handicrafts, also collapsed since many farmers were also craftspeople. At the same time, however, Europe's city-dwellers became interested in the natural beauty of the mountains. Inspired by a romantic vision of the mountain environment, tourism began to take off in the 1880s.

Europe's Playground

Today, tourism is the strongest economic force in the Alps. About 100 million people visit the Alps every year. In money terms, the Alps earn about 25 percent of the entire world's tourist business.

Without tourism, it is safe to say that the Alps would have lost most of their inhabitants in the 1900s. Although very few parts of the Alps have been untouched by human hands, under traditional methods they were managed in a way that avoided environmental damage. For example, the shepherds who tended steep alpine pastures helped prevent **landslides** and erosion.

Tourism has brought its own set of problems to the Alps. Skiing has become extremely popular since the 1960s. The result has been increased deforestation as slopes are cleared of trees to make way for ski lifts and for downhill ski trails. Buildings are put up to accommodate the tourists and roads are built to carry in people and supplies. The result has been an increase in soil, water, and air pollution.

Left: A chairlift stands empty on this alpine ski slope after the snow has melted. Clearing slopes of their vegetation is likely to result in erosion. This in turn can cause landslides.

THE ROCKY MOUNTAINS

The Rocky Mountains stretch north-south across two of the world's leading industrial economies, the United States and Canada. Unlike the Alps, the Rockies were never extensively farmed or settled, even by the original inhabitants of North America, the Indians.

Explorers in the early 1800s named the Rockies for their rugged appearance. They were regarded mainly as a troublesome barrier to the settlers who, in the mid-1800s, moved in huge numbers to a new life on the Pacific coast.

Gold Rush Mountains

The discovery of gold in the Rockies in 1858 created a gold rush that became a major force in the region's economic development. In spite of this, the mountains are still only sparsely populated, with less than two million permanent residents.

Despite the small population, the Rockies today play an important role in North American life. Forestry is a major industry, and significant deposits of copper, gold, lead, and molybdenum are mined. Approximately one-fourth of the water supply in the United States has its source in the Rockies.

Hundreds of thousands of tourists visit the area's many national parks to enjoy the scenery. Skiing is also a major attraction. With so many visitors, the parks can be overcrowded during the summer vacation season. In some popular valleys, exhaust fumes from cars become trapped between the steep mountain walls, causing serious air pollution.

Nature Takes its Course

Some of the best-known national parks in the United States, including Yellowstone and the Tetons, are found in the Rockies. They are renowned for their wild beauty. National parks elsewhere in the world often have allowed the native people who live in the area to continue their traditional

Above: Molas Lake near Silverton, Colorado, in the Rockies. This huge mountain system extends from New Mexico, through Canada, to Alaska. The U.S. Rockies alone have more than 20 mountain ranges.

Left: Most of Yellowstone National Park is situated in northwestern Wyoming. The average height of the park is 8,000 feet (2,500 m), and the whole area is volcanic.

lifestyle. But many U.S. parks have had less human interference. Not everyone agrees that less human interference is good. For example, park authorities have a policy of not putting out natural fires, since they are part of the **ecological cycle.** But in 1988, when fires engulfed almost half of Yellowstone's two million acres (800,000 hectares), some people accused the park services of letting the matter get out of hand.

THE HIMALAYA

The world's largest mountain area, the Himalaya, lies in central Asia. The Himalaya and the surrounding mountain ranges contain most of the world's highest peaks. Apart from Mount Everest, there are 12 other peaks over 26,250 feet (8,000 m). To the north of the Himalaya lies the vast plateau of Tibet. The lives of 500 million people in the lowland plains to the south depend on the waters of the Himalaya, which feed the Ganges, Brahmaputra, and Indus Rivers.

The Himalayan territory is shared by eight nations. Although the mountains are hard to reach, they have had a history of wars and invasion. As a result, a huge variety of people live in the area. Islam, Hinduism, and Buddhism are the main religions.

Below: Harvesttime in a village in Tibet. The Tibetan summer is hot but short. The climate is very cold for the rest of the year. Formerly an independent country, Tibet is now a self-governing region of China.

The people share a way of life that has changed little over hundreds of years. They depend on rearing hardy livestock, such as sheep, goats, horses, and yaks. They also grow crops on the few small areas of fertile soil.

Mountain Farmers

The most densely populated parts of the Himalaya are in the low-altitude southern valleys. Here the climate is mild and the soil so fertile that the land can support large numbers of people. Plentiful crops of grain and fruit are harvested. Almost all the land is cultivated, in fields and terraces. Little of the original vegetation remains.

Above: Yaks are used for plowing in the mountains and on the high plateau of Tibet. Their thick coats help protect them from the cold. They have a large heart and lungs, which help them breathe oxygen from the thin mountain air. Yaks are members of the ox family and are related to the North American bison.

Right: Eastern Himalayan forests, such as this one in Bhutan, are home to many wild animals, including musk deer, gorals, serows, takins, and red pandas. These are the prey of the leopard, wolf, and Himalayan black bear.
 Farther west, where less rain falls, the forest is not as thick and cannot support as many kinds of animals. Throughout the Himalaya, forests like this are dying out.

On the inhospitable higher slopes, the human population is much smaller. The people grow all their own food in the few places that are suitable for crops and livestock. They live in small villages close to their fields, and large areas remain uninhabited.

Yaks are well suited to help people survive in the high mountains of central Asia. The domestic yak was originally bred from its wild ancestor about 1,000 years ago. The wild yak is now almost extinct. The yak serves people by providing them with milk, meat, leather, and wool. Yaks are also used to carry heavy loads and to pull plows. When wood is scarce, dried yak dung is used for fuel.

THE MOUNTAINS OF AFRICA

The high mountains of Africa are scattered and isolated from each other. Close to the equator, Mount Kilimanjaro (19,340 ft/5,895 m) rises to its snowy peak from the surrounding low-lying grasslands. Not all the African mountains are high enough to have permanent snow. But many reach an alpine zone, and most have a forest zone.

Above: Mount Kilimanjaro, Africa's highest mountain, is an extinct volcano. The highest parts of the mountain are a cold desert. The summit is covered by snow and ice. The glaciers have been disappearing rapidly as Africa's climate becomes drier.

Forests Catch the Rain
African mountain forests are important sources of rivers and streams. Mosses and leaves that have fallen from forest trees absorb the flow of water, slowing it down. This process protects the soil from erosion and prevents floods. The farmers who live on the lower mountain slopes rely on this supply of water.

In Africa, mountain life has many advantages. The climate is cooler and there is more rainfall than in the hot, dry lowlands. As a result, mountain areas are home to much higher populations than the lowlands. For instance, in Kenya, about 60 percent of the country's 28.3 million inhabitants live in the highlands. In Ethiopia, 88 percent of a population of 56 million live in the highland areas, which contain 90 percent of the country's farmland.

Most African mountain dwellers live off mixed farming. They grow grains, such as sorghum and maize, and many kinds of fruits and vegetables. They keep domestic animals such as chickens, goats, and cows.

Population growth

In recent years, heavy population growth has put enormous pressure on the land. People need land to grow food. They need forests to supply firewood. They need clean rivers for drinking water. With more people, there are fewer resources to go around. People get desperate and farm the land too much. In doing so, they use up the soil's nutrients and cause soil erosion. And as people cut down more forest for fuel and for farmland, they have less wood to burn in the future.

Above: Bisoke Crater, in one of the Virunga volcanoes of Rwanda. Volcanoes are cone-shaped mountains. They form when molten rock from deep within the earth pours up to the surface through cracks in the crust. The soils that form on volcanic mountains are often very fertile and are much sought after for cultivation.

Below: Cattle graze beside a village on the high plateau of Ethiopia. Much of the forest has been cut down to create farmland. Once 80 percent forested, Ethiopia's highlands were only 5 percent forested by the 1990s.

TRIBAL PEOPLES OF NEW GUINEA

New Guinea is a large tropical island to the north of Australia. In the center of New Guinea, forested mountains hide fertile valleys. Until the 1930s, these valleys were isolated from the rest of the world. Here, the people's way of life has survived unchanged for thousands of years.

The people of New Guinea did not know how to make metal tools until the 1900s. Instead, they made tools from other materials, such as wood, bone, shells, bark, leaves, and stone. In most parts of the world such a culture died out thousands of years ago. It still survives in some parts of New Guinea.

A Warlike People

The highlanders of New Guinea have traditionally waged tribal war. Each tribe defended its land from its neighbors. In this way, the tribe ensured that it had enough land to grow food for all its people. Wars did not last long. Few people died but their deaths had to be avenged. It was dangerous to trespass on a neighboring tribe's land. For this reason, tribes were isolated and fiercely independent. This spirit of independence is common to mountain peoples all over the world.

Right: The highlanders of New Guinea traditionally resisted contacts with outsiders. This man belongs to the Huli tribe, first encountered by people from the outside world in 1938. His wig is made from human hair, cut from the heads of his wife and children.

Left: Pigs are not native to New Guinea. They were originally brought in as livestock in the distant past. Since then they have multiplied and many have run wild. The people also keep them as a source of meat. The pigs are usually killed and eaten on ceremonial occasions, such as weddings or the harvest of crops. Every few years in the highlands of southwestern New Guinea, many pigs are killed together in one ceremony. Then the people gorge themselves with pork.

Changing Traditions

The people of New Guinea live mostly in the fertile valleys that suit their favorite crop, the yam or sweet potato. Some valleys get plenty of rain. In others, the gardens are irrigated. There are many different tribes, each with its own language, folklore, and ceremonial costumes.

Now that the outside world has reached these people, their unique culture is changing. Most tribes have abandoned many of their customs. Traditional costumes are being replaced by western clothing.

Previously, the tribes traded in pigs, cassowaries (large ostrich-like forest birds), and feathers. They did not use money. Now, the people want to buy western goods, and they need money to do so. To earn the money, they stop growing their own food and instead raise **cash crops** such as coffee, which they can sell to make a profit. They also sell the trees in their forests to lumber companies.

In this way, much of the tribal knowledge about how to make the best use of the environment is forgotten. Traditional customs prevented people from having many children. Now the population is increasing, which puts greater pressure on the land.

Although they are primarily farmers, the tribespeople still hunt wild animals and gather useful plants from the forest. They know a great deal about the wildlife, which is central to their folklore. The feathers of many birds are used to make beautiful costumes for traditional ceremonies. The feathers of birds of paradise, New Guinea eagles, and some parrots are favorite choices.

As the people become more numerous, they clear more forest. The use of shotguns makes hunting much easier, and wildlife numbers decline. There are fewer birds to provide feathers for costumes. To help increase wildlife, the government of Papua New Guinea has set up the Siwi-Utame Wildlife Management Area. Here, the people protect the land and its wildlife by traditional methods, and the numbers of wildlife are now increasing again.

Above: This valley in New Guinea has been cleared to create land for traditional agriculture. For centuries, the forested mountains and deep valleys kept the tribes isolated from each other as well as from the outside world. As a result, there are still hundreds of different languages and dialects.

THREATS TO THE MOUNTAINS

Over the past 50 years, mountains have become more accessible. This situation is partly due to modern engineering methods. Roads now reach even the most forbidding mountain ranges. The Karakoram Highway, completed in 1978, now links Pakistan to China along the Khunjerab Pass (14,928 ft/4,550 m). So difficult and dangerous was the construction that nearly 500 people lost their lives while building the highway.

Many new roads in mountainous areas are built for military purposes. To defend their frontiers, nations build routes to help their armies reach the borders easily. Roads are also built to develop trade between countries and to enable lowland people to reach the forests and minerals of the mountains.

Inevitably, roads bring change. New people come to settle in the mountains. Tourists visit them for pleasure. And mountain people move from their homes to lowland cities, where job opportunities are better. In this way, traditional patterns of life for people, for forests, and for wildlife give way to new ones. Often, this process causes destruction.

Above: Fire is commonly used to clear land for cultivation. Here, on Mount Oku in Cameroon, farmers clear forested land for gardens. Fires that get out of control can destroy even more forest.

Left: The people of the Himalaya in Nepal depend on firewood for cooking. Formerly, only deadwood was collected. Nowadays, there are so many people that there is not enough deadwood, so living trees are cut for firewood. This practice is destroying the forests.

Dams and Electricity

Another major engineering threat to mountains is the hydroelectric dam. Mountain valleys are attractive to dam-builders. The valleys usually have a plentiful supply of water. If the valley is steep sided, it is relatively easy to build a dam across. Compared to the lowlands, mountain areas also often have fewer inhabitants. The small population makes it easier to resettle people when a new dam floods their homes. But in the process, communities are uprooted, forests are destroyed, and farmland is flooded.

Dams are designed to generate hydroelectricity and sometimes to store water for irrigation. But mountain areas pay a heavy price for this. In the Alps, not one major river flows for its entire course in a natural condition. Fewer than ten major Alpine rivers flow uninterrupted for more than 9 miles (15 km). In many other Alpine valleys, plans have been made to build dams that will turn the valleys into reservoirs, or lakes, to store water.

Changing climate

Mountains, by their very height, create their own climate. Climates also change over time. The last Ice Age ended about 10,000 years ago. Then the climate grew warmer. During the past century, the speed at which the climate has begun to get warmer has increased. Mountain glaciers in the Alps and the Rocky Mountains have been shrinking.

These changes may be natural. Many scientists, however, believe that human activities have changed the climate. For example, the glaciers on Mount Kilimanjaro have shrunk greatly during the 1900s. The African climate has become drier, and less snow is falling to replenish the ice.

Above: In the Andes of Bolivia, even steep slopes are cultivated. Such cultivation can be harmful to the soil. These women are harvesting coca, the leaves of which are chewed as a drug. Long ago, such steep slopes would not have been tilled.

DYING CULTURES

Many distinctive cultures were once protected from change by the remoteness of the mountains. Today, these cultures are being replaced by new customs that often conflict with traditional practices.

We have already seen how traditional knowledge of the mountains allowed people to make intelligent use of their environment without damaging it. This knowledge enabled them to continue living in the same way for hundreds of years.

In Tibet, people survived by the careful use of scarce resources, so they would not use up anything they needed from the land. This balance was difficult to achieve because the land does not produce much. In order to control their population, they practiced **polyandry,** a custom in which one woman marries several men. This allows the population to stay the same size instead of growing.

Cash Crops

The introduction of money may bring change faster than anything else. People are attracted by consumer goods, but they need money to purchase them. They stop growing their own food and instead grow cash crops to sell on the international market. This earns them

Right: An elderly Quechua Indian wearing traditional costume. These people come from the mountains of Peru, South America. Many of them have abandoned their traditional dress and lifestyle and have moved to lowland towns and cities. There, they have been treated unfairly by the lowland people already living in the cities.

the money they need to buy manufactured goods. But tasks that had been carried out by the community as a whole, such as maintaining terraces, start to be neglected. Individuals are too busy dealing with their cash crops.

As traditional practices are abandoned, an irreversible process is begun. Terraces, for example, represent a huge investment of time and labor made over hundreds of years. If the terraces are not maintained, they rapidly fall into disrepair. As a result, people become more dependent than ever on growing crops that earn them cash.

Above: People cultivating the steep slopes of Mount Oku, Cameroon. The forest has been cleared and the soil tilled. Such forest soil will support good crops at first. But the land has not been terraced and heavy rain will wash the soil away. The people will then need to clear more forest in order to make a living.

Below: A scene in Lhasa, capital of Tibet. Before it was taken over by China, Tibet was a Buddhist country with the Dalai Lama as both political and spiritual leader. Since then, many Chinese have moved into Tibet, monasteries have been destroyed, and the traditional culture is under severe threat.

FOREST, SOIL, AND WATER

Without forest or vegetation to hold rain back, the water rushes downhill. On deforested and overcultivated soils in Ethiopia, about 80 percent of the rainfall runs straight off the mountainside. The result is floods in the lowlands. In contrast, well-covered soils soak up more than 90 percent of the rain they receive. They release the rain into streams and rivers more slowly. This process helps to even out the impact of heavy rainfall and ensures that a steady supply of water is available throughout the year.

Steep, deforested slopes are often unstable and landslides are common. The rain takes much of the remaining soil with it. When the soil is gone, the land can no longer support the plants, animals, and humans that depend on it. People must then move to the fertile soil protected by the remaining forests.

Problems Downstream

People in the lowlands depend on a stable environment in the mountains. The fertile soil washed down from the mountains is deposited as silt in the lowlands. In the past, if the floods were gentle, the silt would help keep farmland fertile in the lowlands. One farmer described it like this: "Earlier the flood came silently like a small cat,

SOIL EROSION

The mountain people of Nepal build terraces in order to grow crops on steep slopes. Without terraces, rain easily washes away the soil. This land was formerly forested and the last trees are still standing. They will eventually die. The people cut the branches for firewood. They take the leaves to feed their livestock.

The eroded soil will grow only poor pastures. In order to survive, the people will need to move on and clear more forest. The human population is growing so fast that it is difficult to stop this type of soil erosion.

Left: Until recently, seasonal floods were welcomed by the people of Bangladesh, in the lowlands below the Himalaya. The floods brought silt and water that fertilized their farmland. But the mountain forests, which once held back the floods, are dwindling. Soil washed down from the mountains is choking the rivers. The floods are now out of control. Once they brought life, now they bring death. Thousands of people have lost their lives. Many more have lost their livelihoods.

Below: The Incas, who inhabited the high Andes for many centuries, had strict rules to protect soil from erosion. After Spanish conquerors defeated the Incas in the 1500s, their practices were forgotten. Soil erosion, seen here in Bolivia, has now become a common sight.

touched our feet, and went away in a few days, giving us fertile **silt.** Now it comes with the speed of a tiger, takes away everything, covers the land with sand, and does not go away."

In the lower reaches of the Ganges River in Bangladesh, for instance, floods have become increasingly destructive as forests are destroyed in the Himalaya. The result is the loss of thousands of lives and great damage to property. So much silt has been washed down the Ganges that a large island is forming beyond its mouth in the Bay of Bengal.

THE TROUBLE WITH TOURISM

Because of their beauty and the challenge they offer to climbers, some mountains are very popular with tourists. This can be of benefit to mountain areas. Tourists spend money, which provides income and employment for local residents. But tourism can also bring problems.

Tourists often destroy the very thing they come to see. This has been described as "loving it to death." Although the mountains themselves are hard to change, their vegetation, wildlife, and cultures are very fragile. Even well-meaning visitors can cause permanent damage.

Trekkers in Nepal

A good example of this problem is the Khumbu Valley in Nepal. At the head of the valley lies Mount Everest, and every year about 10,000 tourists visit the region. Some will be climbers aiming to scale Mount Everest. Most will be trekkers, there to enjoy hiking in the beautiful mountains.

Tourism has brought wealth to the valley. It has also brought disaster to the juniper forests. Trekkers from wealthy parts of the world expect hot water and hot food on their vacation. Formerly, the inhabitants of the Khumbu Valley, the Sherpas, only used dead wood for fuel. Now the demand for firewood has forced them to cut live trees for themselves and the visitors.

People hoped that the juniper forests would grow back. But Sherpas use the extra wealth they get from tourism to buy more livestock. The herds of grazing sheep, goats, and yaks prevent new growth from getting big.

Some visitors also leave their rubbish behind. In the cold climate, especially above the snow line, garbage does not rot away. Mountaineers have left at least 30 tons of trash on Mount Everest alone.

Above: Tourists in the forested Andes of Ecuador. For people from wealthy countries, vacations in faraway places are now popular. More and more people want to visit wild and remote locations. But uncontrolled tourism can seriously change the way of life of the local people.

SHERPA PORTERS IN NEPAL

Many mountaineers visit the Himalaya each year to climb the high peaks. To carry their equipment, food, and other supplies they hire porters. These are usually local people. They burn the scarce wood and the alpine cushion plants that take a long time to grow. The porters work for money, which replaces their traditional activities. In time they forget these traditions.

Right: Erosion in the Kaligandaki Valley in Nepal, near Mount Annapurna. A section of a trail has collapsed into the valley. When there are too many visitors, the vegetation of the remote valleys near the high peaks is likely to suffer.

THE FUTURE OF MOUNTAINS

Only one in every ten people in the world lives in mountains. But five out of every ten people depend on mountains in some way. Mountains help supply our water and influence our weather. They provide us with power, with lumber, and with other useful resources. They contain unique species of plants and animals. We enjoy the purity and beauty of mountains when we visit them.

People from the lowlands need to recognize the special needs of mountains and their inhabitants. Many problems in mountain regions are the result of neglect. Politicians usually spend most of their time in lowlands, where most of the population is concentrated. The voices of mountain peoples are far away and easily ignored.

Even when the lowlands suffer from events that begin in mountains, such as river floods, the problem is often misunderstood and the wrong decisions are made. Official attitudes need to change. The disturbance and destruction suffered by the people, the vegetation, and the wildlife of mountains might then stop.

Below: A Buddhist monastery in Bhutan. Boys are admitted at the age of eight and are educated to become monks. Buddhism is a religion that began more than 2,500 years ago in India. Monks spend much of their time praying and studying the teachings of Buddha. To Buddhists, the mountains of the Himalaya are especially holy.

In Nepal and Tibet, the Buddhist culture has been partly replaced by outside influences. To prevent this from happening in Bhutan, the government has restricted the number of foreign visitors.

Above: Women tending tree seedlings in a nursery in Cameroon. One solution to the problem of deforestation is to plant young trees. Many mountain regions now have tree-planting projects. Usually the planting is done by the local people themselves. Planting trees is good, but it is better to protect the forest from destruction in the first place.

Right: A forested mountain valley in Bhutan. More than half of Bhutan is still covered by forest. Such mountain forests are vital for controlling the flow of rainwater as well as for preserving soil and the homes of wildlife. The local people depend on forests.

NATIONAL PARKS

Creating national parks is one way of tackling the problems in mountain regions. Governments have declared some mountainous areas to be national parks so that their beauty and wildlife can be protected. Mounts Everest and Kilimanjaro are both within national parks.

Kilimanjaro National Park is very popular. Up to 15,000 visitors come each year to climb to the summit. They bring a great deal of money to Tanzania. Local people realize that tourists will keep coming only if the area is well preserved. In some national parks, people are charged just for the privilege of visiting them. Fees to climb Mount Everest are very high. The Nepalese charge more than $7,500 per person for climbing the mountain.

Sagarmatha National Park
Mount Everest is called Sagarmatha by the Sherpas of the Khumbu Valley in Nepal. Their national park has the same name. Sherpas have begun to return to the traditional method of protecting the forest. They call this system *shinga nawa*. Inspectors called *nawas* have the job of checking that people do not harm the forest. Live trees must not be cut and wild animals must not be killed. People caught by the nawas doing wrong are fined.

Some small areas in the park have been planted with trees specially grown to replace the lost forest. The protection of wildlife has helped some species become more plentiful. Musk deer and tahrs were rare when the park was first established. Now there are enough to provide food for the even rarer snow leopard.

Rules for Tourists
Visitors too must follow the rules. Usually, tourists are not permitted to damage any plant or kill any animal. In

Right: Machhapuchhare (22,746 ft/6,933 m) in Nepal is sacred to the Gurung people who live in the valley below. Although it offers a great challenge to mountaineers, no one is allowed to climb it. Machhapuchhare guards the entrance to the Annapurna Sanctuary, a beautiful valley surrounded by seven peaks over 23,000 feet (7,000 m)—part of the Annapurna Conservation Area. Here the local people try to live in harmony with the land and its wildlife. The many visitors must not damage the area.

PARKS OR PEOPLE?

When governments create national parks, they sometimes forget about the people who have traditionally depended on that land. When this happens, conflicts develop between the local people and the conservationists.

Local people may realize that cutting down trees and killing rare animals is wrong. But often they are desperate and have no choice. Another option is to share some of the money earned from parks with the local community.

In the Annapurna Conservation Area of Nepal, for instance, trekkers are charged the equivalent of $15 a day to walk there. Much of this money is spent to improve conditions such as sanitation and education in the local community. Fuel-efficient facilities for tourists are another example of the way the income is spent. In this way, the visitors can keep coming without causing further destruction of forests for firewood.

Left: Ama Dablam (22,495 ft/6,856 m) in Sagarmatha National Park, Nepal. It is a holy mountain to the Sherpas who live in its shadow. Sagarmatha National Park was set up in 1976 to protect the scenery, wilderness, and culture around Mount Everest.

Nepal, visitors should not use the scarce firewood, which is needed by the local people. Instead, they can cook on camping stoves that burn kerosene.

Holy Places

All over the world, mountains have been worshipped in the beliefs and customs of traditional people. For Christian and Jewish people, Mount Sinai is a holy place. They believe it is where Moses received the Ten Commandments from God. For the Hindus, the Himalaya are the abode of the gods. The Buddhist religion teaches care for the land, its vegetation, and its wildlife.

A New Start

Not everyone is religious. But when we see the damage that has been done to mountains, we can see the sense in these beliefs. If mountains are not to suffer from further destruction, people must learn to treat them with respect again.

Although destruction continues, much has been learned from the mistakes of the past. People have started to repair the damage. Forests are being protected and replanted. Inhabitants are getting help in preserving their ancient customs.

Glossary

acid rain: Rainfall that contains chemical pollutants from the air. When combined with water, these pollutants form acids than can harm plants, animals, and habitats.

alpine meadow: A zone of pastureland above the tree line in mountainous areas.

altiplano: A high-altitude plateau, or plain. A tableland.

altitude: Height above sea level.

block mountains: Steep-sided mountains, created by the rise and fall of land between fault lines (cracks in the earth's crust).

cash crop: A crop such as coffee, cocoa beans, or fruit that is grown by people for sale rather than for their own use.

crust (of the earth): The solidified layer of rock on the earth's outer surface.

deforestation: The large-scale cutting or burning of trees in a forest, either for timber or to clear land for farming.

ecological cycle: The natural renewal of living things in a particular environment.

erosion: The wearing away of the earth's surface by wind, water, or ice.

fold mountains: Mountains formed when moving plates cause the earth's crust to twist or fold over.

glacier: A river of ice that moves slowly down a mountainside.

hydroelectric power: Electricity generated by turbines that are driven by water from a waterfall or a reservoir.

irrigation: The use of water, transported by artificial means such as canals or sprinklers, to enable crops to grow.

landslide: A mass of snow, rocks, or mud sliding down a hillside, often caused by erosion following deforestation.

life zones: Climatic areas at different altitudes on a mountainside, each with its own plants and animals.

migration: The movement of people or animals from one region to another, usually for feeding or breeding.

moraine: A mound of soil, gravel, and rocks carried by a glacier and left behind when the ice melts.

national park: An area of land set aside by a national government to protect plant and animal life.

plateau: An area of level but high land in a mountainous region.

plate: In earth science, a massive slab of the earth's crust that moves very slowly over the molten rock beneath it.

polyandry: A practice in which one woman marries several men, as opposed to polygamy, in which one man marries several women.

rain forest: A thick, wet, evergreen forest found in tropical areas with heavy daily rainfall.

rain shadow: The dry area on the opposite side of a mountain range to that where most of the rain falls.

Sherpa: People of a Buddhist tribe from Nepal, some of whom work as porters for mountaineering expeditions.

silt: Tiny particles of rock carried by rivers and often deposited in low-lying areas.

snout (of a glacier): The front or leading end of a glacier.

terraces: A series of flat platforms (or "steps") dug into a hillside so that crops can be grown. Terraces prevent soil erosion and help water soak into the ground.

transhumance: The movement of livestock from mountain pastures in the summer to valley pastures in the winter.

tree line: On a mountain, the altitude above which no trees will grow.

valley: A long hollow lying between hills or mountains, formed as a river or glacier wears away soil and rock in its path. Mountain valleys are often narrow and steep-sided.

volcano: An opening in the earth's crust through which lava (molten rock) is thrown up (erupted). With each eruption, lava often builds up around the opening, gradually forming a mountain.

Index